J152.46 ORR
Orr, Tamra, author.
Fear

Guelph Public Library

FEELINGS
Fear

Tamra B. Orr

Published in the United States of America
by Cherry Lake Publishing
Ann Arbor, Michigan
www.cherrylakepublishing.com

Reading Adviser: Marla Conn MS, Ed., Literacy specialist, Read-Ability, Inc.

Photo Credits: © Ilike/Shutterstock Images, cover, 1; © Lee Prince/Shutterstock Images, 4; © Daniel Jedzura/Shutterstock Images, 6; © verandah/Shutterstock Images, 8; © Sergey Nivens/Shutterstock Images, 10; © Happy Together/Shutterstock Images, 12; © Annette Shaff/Shutterstock Images, 14; © digitalskillet/iStock Images, 16; © Ryan Kelly/iStock Images, 18; © Ronnachai Palas/Shutterstock Images, 20

Copyright ©2017 by Cherry Lake Publishing
All rights reserved. No part of this book may be reproduced or utilized in any form or by any means without written permission from the publisher.

Library of Congress Cataloging-in-Publication Data
Names: Orr, Tamra, author.
  Title: Fear / Tamra B. Orr.
Description: Ann Arbor : Cherry Lake Publishing, 2016. | Series: Feelings | Audience: K to Grade 3. | Includes bibliographical references and index.
Identifiers: LCCN 2015048117| ISBN 9781634710466 (hardcover) | ISBN 9781634711456 (pdf) | ISBN 9781634712446 (pbk.) | ISBN 9781634713436 (ebook)
Subjects: LCSH: Fear—Juvenile literature.
Classification: LCC BF575.F2 O697 2016 | DDC 152.4/6—dc23
LC record available at http://lccn.loc.gov/2015048117

Cherry Lake Publishing would like to acknowledge the work of The Partnership for 21st Century Learning. Please visit *www.p21.org* for more information.

Printed in the United States of America
Corporate Graphics

Table of Contents

5	Fear
11	In the Dark
15	A Yell
19	Feeling Safe
22	Find Out More
22	Glossary
23	Home and School Connection
24	Index
24	About the Author

4

Fear

Night has come.

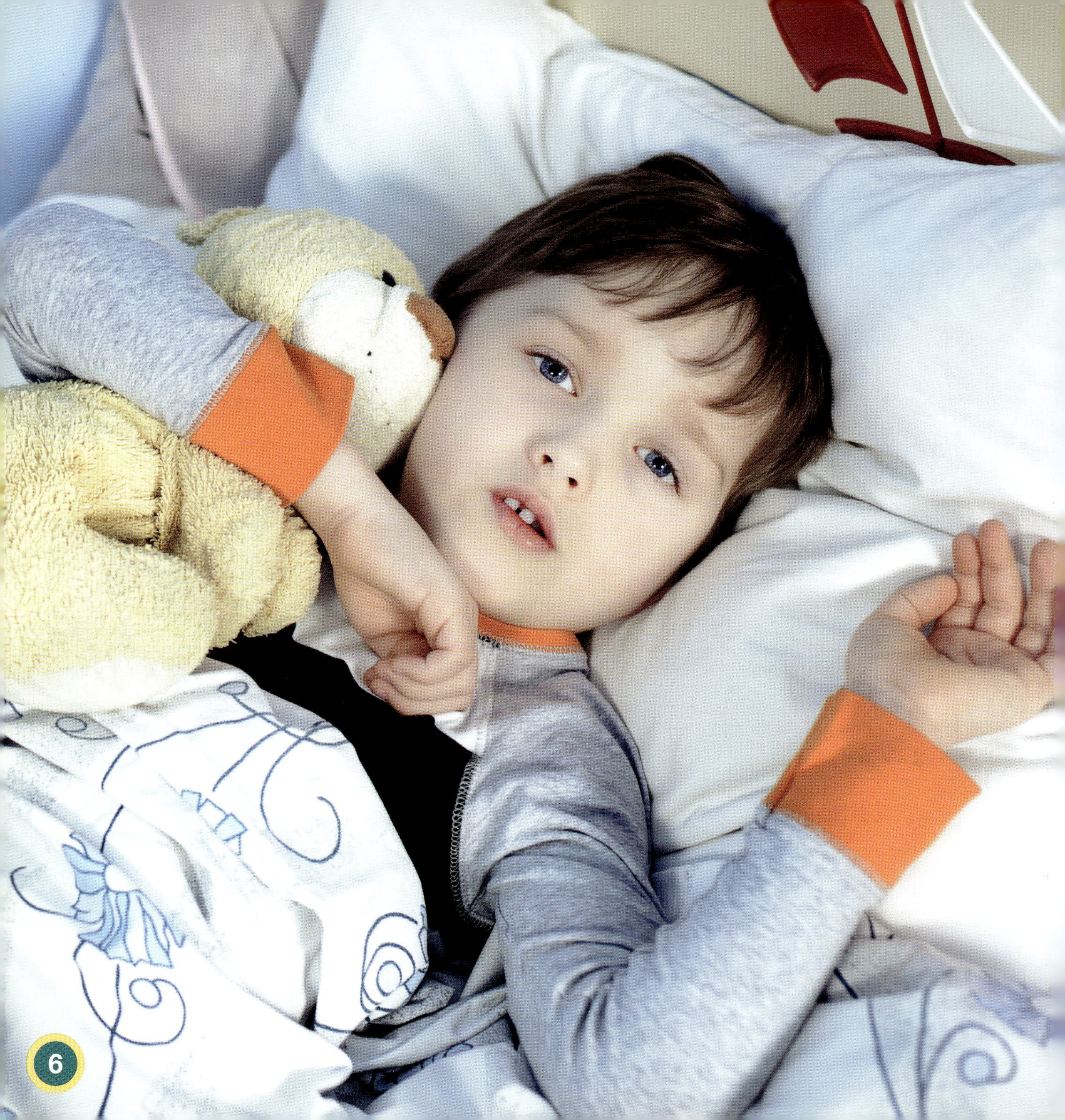

Mom says it is time for bed.

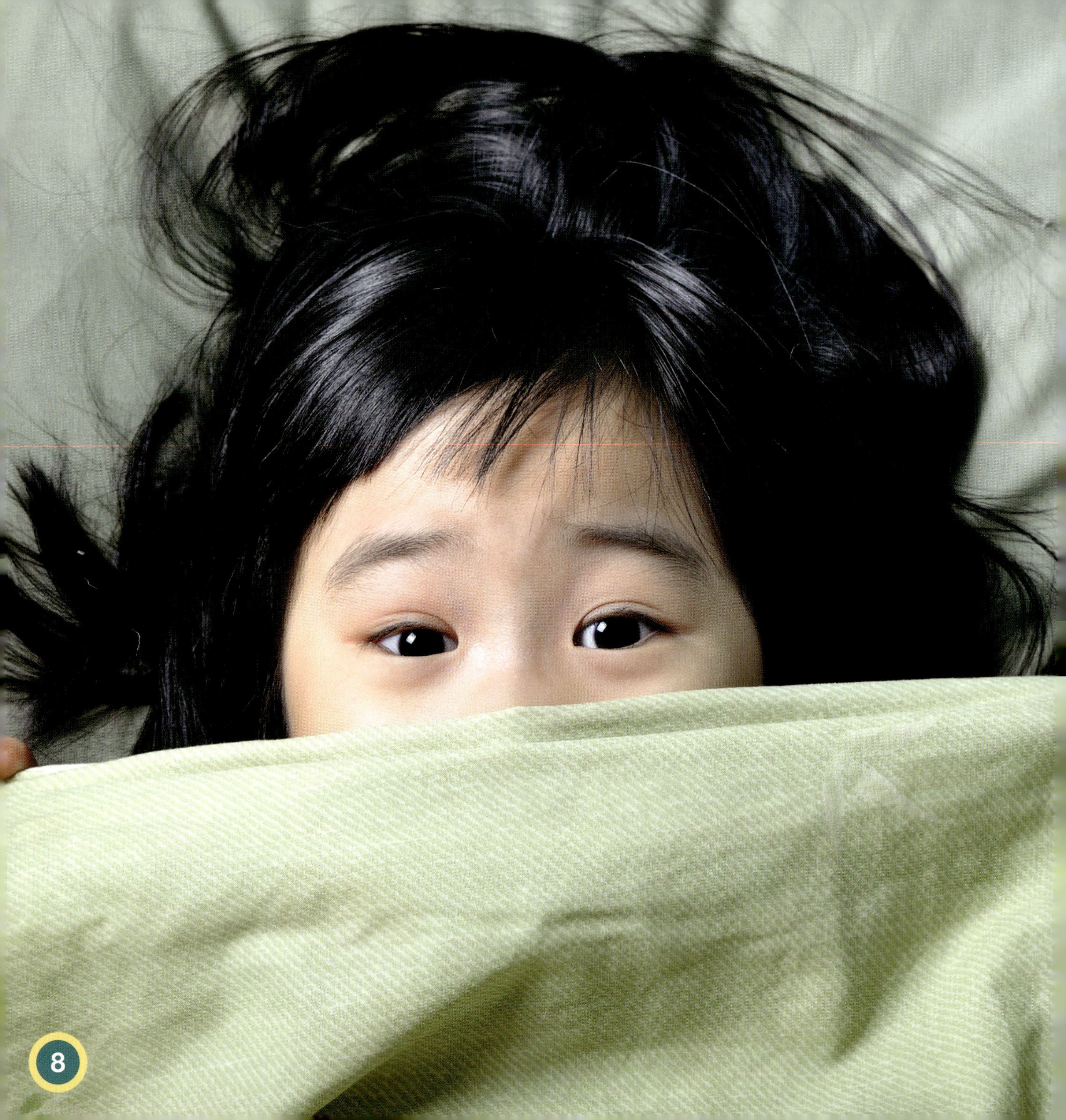

But, Mom! It is too dark to sleep!

I am afraid of the dark.

Why is this boy scared?

10

In the Dark

The dark is full of **shadows**.

Is something hiding under my bed? Or maybe in my **closet**?

12

I go under the **covers**. I can hear my heart.

It **beats** fast and loud with fear.

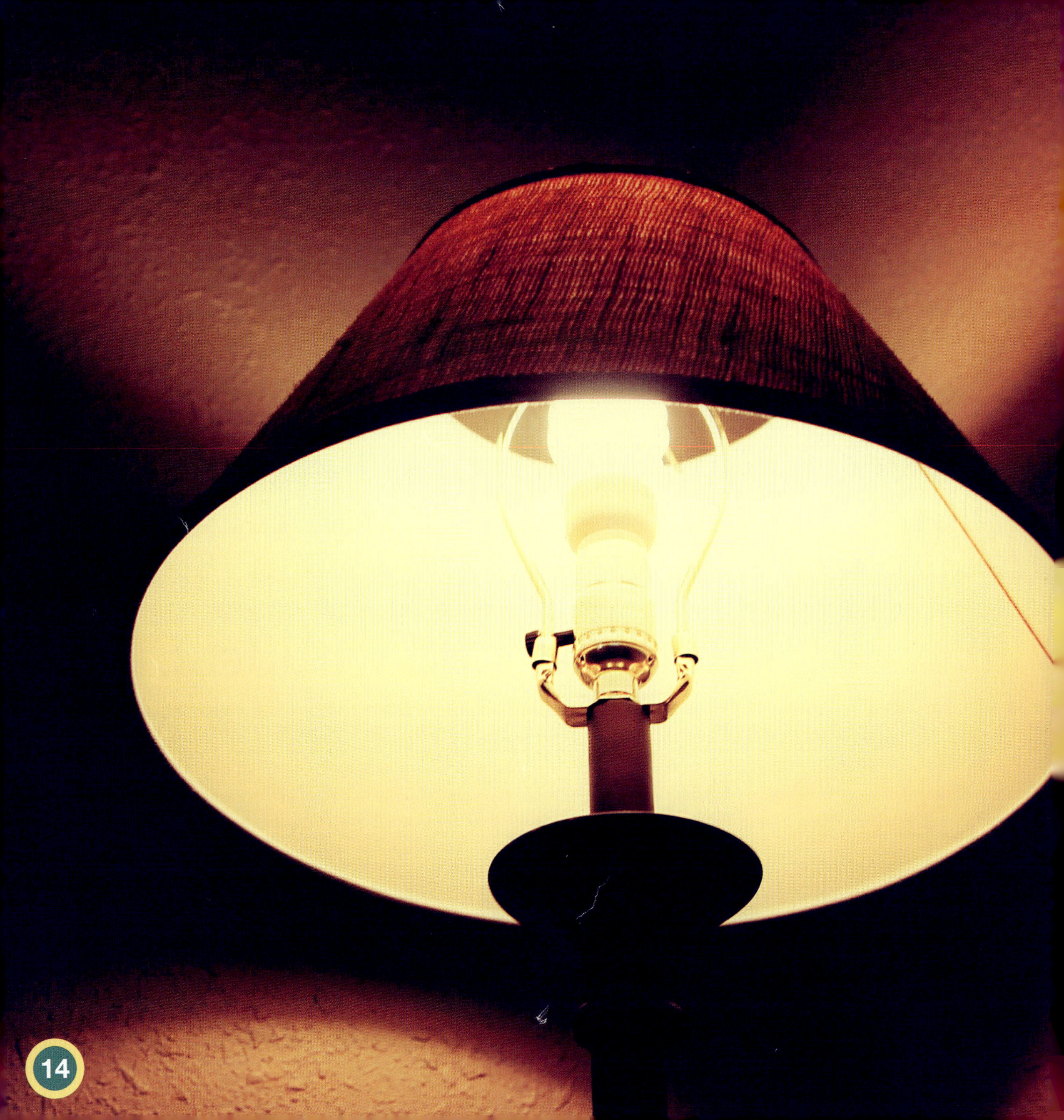

A Yell

I yell. Dad comes. He turns on the light.

He looks in the closet and under the bed.

16

There is nothing there.

But I am still afraid.

18

Feeling Safe

Dad hugs me. He **plugs** in a night-light.

It chases the shadows away.

How is this girl feeling?

I get another hug and smile.
I am safe again.

Find Out More

Graves, Sue. *Who Feels Scared? A Book About Being Afraid*. Minneapolis: Free Spirit Publishing, 2011.

Richards, Dan. *The Problem with Not Being Scared of Monsters.* Honesdale, PA: Boyds Mill Press, 2014.

Thomas, Pat. *Why Do I Feel Scared? A First Look at Being Brave*. Hauppauge, NY: Barron's Educational Series, 2010.

Glossary

beats (BEETS) pounds in a regular rhythm
closet (KLAH-zit) a place to hang clothing
covers (KUHV-urz) blankets
plugs (PLUHGZ) connects with electricity
shadows (SHAD-ohz) dark shapes

Home and School Connection

Use this list of words from the book to help your child become a better reader. Word games and writing activities can help beginning readers reinforce literacy skills.

afraid	fear	nothing
again	for	plugs
and	full	safe
another	get	says
away	has	shadows
beats	hear	sleep
bed	heart	smile
but	hiding	something
can	hug	still
chases	hugs	the
closet	light	there
come	looks	time
comes	loud	too
covers	maybe	turns
dad	mom	under
dark	night	with
fast	night-light	yell

Index

bed, 7, 11, 15

closet, 11, 15
covers, 13

dad, 15, 19
dark, 9, 11

heart, 13

light, 15

mom, 7, 9

night, 5

night-light, 19

shadows, 11, 19
sleep, 9

About the Author

Tamra Orr has written more than 400 books for young people. The only thing she loves more than writing books is reading them. She lives in beautiful Portland, Oregon, with her husband, four children, dog, and cat. She says that even as a grown-up, she, too, is a bit afraid of the dark.